ACROSS
THE
PLAINS

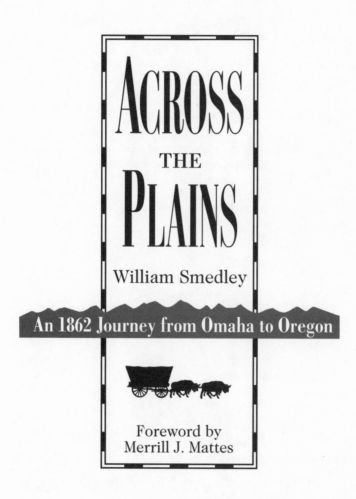

ACROSS THE PLAINS

William Smedley

An 1862 Journey from Omaha to Oregon

Foreword by
Merrill J. Mattes

JOHNSON BOOKS: BOULDER

Cover and text design: Margaret Donharl

Library of Congress Cataloging-in-Publication Data
Smedley, William, 1836–1926
    [Across the Plains in '62]
    Across the plains : an 1862 journey from Omaha to Oregon / William Smedley ; foreword by Merrill J. Mattes.
       p. cm.
    Originally published: Across the plains in '62. Denver, Colo., 1916.
    ISBN 1-55566-123-8
    1. West (U.S.)—Description and travel. 2. Overland journeys to the Pacific. 3. Oregon Trail. 4. West (U.S.)—History—1860–1890. 5. Smedley, William, 1836–1926—Diaries. 6. Pioneers—West (U.S.)—Diaries. I. Title.
F594.S65   1994
917.804'33'092—dc20
[B]   93-49833
                                      CIP

1 2 3 4 5 6 7 8 9

Printed in the United States of America by
Johnson Printing Company
1880 South 57th Court
Boulder, Colorado 80301

In 1862, William Smedley, a twenty-six-year-old school teacher originally from West Chester, Pennsylvania, embarked from Illinois on one of his life's great adventures. With apparently little forethought, he set out to cross the Great Plains and the Rocky Mountains and travel to Oregon. The yellowed pages of the diary he kept of this trek were first published by his family in 1916.

Over the years, the little book became a treasured keepsake for William Smedley's growing number of descendants, and passages from it were frequently read at family weddings, christenings, and funerals. Our long association with Carl Blaurock, one of Colorado's eminent mountaineers and first cousin of Max Giesecke—who was William Smedley's son-in-law—introduced us to the Smedley family. Nelson Giesecke, Max's grandson, asked us if the diary had a market outside of the family. We read it with great interest and answered with an enthusiastic "yes!"

Distinguished Western historian Merrill J. Mattes, recognized authority on the interpretation of diaries by emigrants following both sides of the Platte, agreed to write a foreword. What follows the foreword is a reprint of the 1916 printing of Smedley's diary.

The Publisher

David W. Culp

William Smedley

Foreword

In Platte River Road Narratives I award William Smedley three stars for his account of his adventurous 1862 journey from Illinois to Oregon. Requested by his descendent, my fellow Littleton Rotarian Bob Smedley, to write a foreword for this new edition of Smedley's 1916 volume, and thus having an opportunity to read it once more, I would be tempted now to award him four stars, for the thoroughness and quality of his narrative. I am further impressed with its credibility and literary merit, reflecting actual trail happenings, including a fair share of melodrama.

Quite recently, Bob Smedley discovered the original ancestral Smedley diary at the Colorado Historical Society. My subsequent examination of it indicated that the 1916 publication was essentially the same as the original. What is amazing about the original diary is its size—a tiny leather-bound booklet only slightly larger than two by three inches, with sixteen lines per page, written in tiny script but still legible, even without the help of a magnifying glass. Equally interesting is the realization that this young writer was not really a bona fide "emigrant," but a young adventurer! Despite the hardships and dangers of his journey, William Smedley managed to write a complete and coherent record of his 1862 transcontinental trek.

The sesquicentennial of the original Oregon Trail of 1843 has given the public a new understanding and appreciation of the historical importance of all westward migrations up what I call the "Great Platte River Road" in my first book, or more precisely, the "Great Platte Valley Migration Corridor of 1843–1866." While both scholarly and popular authors tend to focus on the much heralded early migrations of 1843–1853 to Oregon and California, the later years up through 1866 have suffered neglect. The reality is that the migrations of the later period, 1858–1866, from the Pikes Peak gold rush to the advent of a transcontinental railroad, are of equal importance to those of the more publicized earlier period, but they have been outshone by the glamour of the early Oregon Trail and the epic California gold rush. William Smedley helps to illuminate this somewhat neglected later period.

Attention is called to the rich contribution Smedley has made to our understanding of the overland experience of the still adventurous 1860s, most importantly, his illumination of the misunderstood fact that while the classic Oregon Trail of the 1840s was confined to the south side of the Platte, from 1849 on through the 1860s a fair percentage of people migrating to both California and Oregon traveled along the north side of the Platte, as did Smedley. Until publication of my *Great Platte River Road*, textbooks and popular histories almost uniformly made reference to, and were accompanied by maps showing, "Oregon Trail" along the south side of the Platte, and "Mormon Trail" along the north side. The profusion of recently discovered non-Mormon diaries that reflect heavy travel along the north side of the Platte requires an important revision of emigration history. This long hidden fact is that the California gold rush from 1849 onward, and indeed the migrations to Oregon and adjacent territories through 1866, happened along the north side as well as the south side of the Platte. In my books, for the first time, the south side is finally recognized as "Oregon Trail/California Trail," while the north side is upgraded to "Mormon Trail/ Council Bluffs Road." With recent federal recognition of the California National Historic Trail along the north side of the Platte, the north side route could more legitimately be called the "Mormon Trail/California Trail."

William Smedley provides a brief glimpse of what trials and tribulations awaited the traveler on the north side of the river and beyond in 1862—a journey which, in his words, he would "never regret having passed through nor ever desire to repeat."

Merrill J. Mattes, September 10, 1993

William Smedley

Introduction

$\mathcal{T}$he manuscript from which this little book was taken is in reality a diary kept by William Smedley on his trip across the Plains fifty-four years ago. It had lain on the shelf many long years, until the ink had quite faded. The inspiration for its publication came five years ago, when it was resurrected during a search for material in preparing the banquet to Dr. Smedley on the occasion of his seventy-fifth birthday, May 4, 1911. He was twenty-six years of age at the time of these interesting experiences. He had come to Illinois from his former home near West Chester, Pennsylvania, a year or so before to teach school. As a boy he was afflicted with bronchitis and was of a stature that did not promise a sturdy physique for manhood.

This long trip of two thousand miles from Omaha City to Salem, Oregon, five months of time, was accomplished with ox teams over the "Oregon Trail," and is nearly the same route which now takes but two days with the modern express trains. It was the route which the greater number of brave pioneers who then peopled the great Northwest had taken. It followed the valleys of the Platte, the Sweet Water and Snake rivers and many other streams, and crossed the main range of the Rocky Mountains, the Blue Mountains and the Cascades south of Mount Hood. The incidents recorded

reveal the experiences with Indians, both friendly
and hostile, and the necessity for a constant state of
preparedness for surprise attacks by stage coach bandits.
Fraught with danger, as was this long journey to the far
western country, it also had its pleasures and attractions.
At times pestered with mosquitoes and the biting dust
of the plains, they also had the beautiful sunsets and
sunrises and the brisk, stimulating air of the mountain
region. While the greater part of the time he and his
partner traveled by themselves, they, at times, joined
other caravans and shared their conveniences and
responsibilities. The various landmarks were eagerly
looked for and the final goal was a hope that only those
of a determined spirit can appreciate. There was no
time to think of illness, and as they pushed farther and
farther from the civilization they had left they adapted
themselves to the situation and covered the fifteen to
twenty-five miles a day without a thought or possibility
of retreat.

He taught school near Salem for one year. From
there he went to Portland and took a boat for San
Francisco, touching, as was the custom in those days,
at Vancouver, B.C. From San Francisco he went by
boat to Panama, crossed the Isthmus on the primitive
railroad and returned by boat to New York.

It was not until after this overland trip that he took up the subject of dentistry, graduating March 1st, 1866, at Pennsylvania College of Dental Surgery, coming to Denver in 1870, in which place he has continued to practice for forty-six years, seeing it grow from a town of 4,000 to that of 225,000 inhabitants.

E. R. WARNER. Denver, Colo., June 15, 1916

Chimney Rock

Diary

The spring of 1862 found me as usual in ill health. Having heard much of the salubrity of the Pacific climate I had long desired to visit its coast and this spring, there being some excitement in Salmon River gold mines, almost en route for Oregon, and as a company of Illinois farmers were starting for that place, I determined to start, too, for the gold region, thence to Oregon.

On the 5th day of May I left my Illinois friends and took the cars for Fulton, on the *Mississippi*. The river at this time had quite o'erspread the limits assigned it by nature and extended far out over the adjoining country, almost submerging the railroad in places.

May 6. At seven P.M. took a packet going south. The night was clear, moonlight, beautiful. The broad bosom of the "Father of Waters" was spread out like a silvery sheet before us. Some five or six intelligent, pious-looking Germans assembled on the hurricane deck and enchanted us with the most delightful vocal music I thought I had ever heard. To me there is no music more charming than the singing of German hymns. A moonlight scene on the Mississippi is, of itself, magnificent and the music rendered it perfectly sublime.

May 8. Passed Nauvoo, the deserted city of the Mormons, on a beautiful site on the left bank of the river. Our progress down the river was rather slow as of the previous day, our boat having been much detained taking on freight, it being designed more for that purpose than for the accommodation of passengers. It is astonishing the amount of freight they pile upon these river boats; bringing their guards to the water's edge.

Arrived at Hannibal in the evening. Here we found ourselves under military regulations; baggage must be inspected and firearms delivered over to the baggage master. Forty-eight hours' ride had brought us into a different climate. We left northern Illinois cold, frosty and desolate; here peach trees had bloomed and shed their blossoms.

May 9. Left this morning on the Hannibal & St. Jo. Railroad. The road at this time was under military guard and peace and quiet prevailed along the route, though many signs of hostilities were still to be seen, such as numerous bullet holes through sides of the cars, bullet marks on the engine and ruins of burned bridges.

About twelve hours' ride brought us to St. Joseph, the terminus of the road, which we also found under military law. This place, once a trading post kept by one St. Joseph, a Canadian Frenchman, is one of the outfitting points for emigrants crossing the plains.

May 10. Took the packet *Omaha* for Omaha City. The dark, turbid waters of the Missouri contrast very unfavorably with the bright waters of the Mississippi. Even at this season of the year, when water is supposed to be high, we had much difficulty in ascending this troublesome stream. Snags and sandbars repeatedly arrested our progress. This river is a "grand uncertainty," as "unstable as water." Where the stream flows today in six months may be dry land and the stream have made for itself a new channel. A sudden change will throw the current against a bank, covered with trees that look to have held peaceful possession for years, perhaps for centuries, gradually the soil is crumbled away and one by one the old patriarchs of the forest are undermined and precipitated headlong into the turbid stream, to be floated away or remain a dangerous obstacle to navigation. One peculiar feature that struck me was the numerous deserted villages along the river bank. These I learned were common in the West—wrecks of airy castles of speculators who had bought land upon the river, ofttimes without natural advantages for permanency, built a few houses, drew maps and called them cities. After earnest but fruitless endeavors to induce to the places sufficient enterprise to give them vitality, the experiments were abandoned and the buildings remain as monuments to the founders' ambition and their folly.

May 11. This was the first Sabbath I had spent in a region where its sanctity was entirely disregarded. We seemed to have gotten beyond the realm of devotion. Pistol shooting and other such amusements were resorted to to break the ennui of the occasion.

May 13. Arrived at Omaha about daylight; found the city not upon the river bank, but judiciously built upon the upland about one-half mile distant. This low, intervening flat was perhaps once the bed of the river, and who can say how soon it may be again?

The first striking feature that meets the eyes of the stranger at this time, particularly if he be from the Atlantic states, is the restless, moving throng of emigrants, each armed with a knife upon one side and a revolver upon the other, strung to a belt, with an expression of enterprise, spirit and determination depicted on his rugged countenance.

Omaha City, and Council Bluffs, four miles distant on opposite sides of the river, are the great outfitting posts of the Northwest. Those who start from the States with their own teams usually stop here to lay in provisions, while those who are obliged to purchase entire outfits come here for that purpose. These circumstances tend to make business quite brisk during the few months of emigration, but during other seasons they must collapse very much like Cape May and Atlantic City. But there is a future for these cities. The Pacific Railroad, which will inevitably be, will bring not only emigration through, but permanent settlers to these places, which will, perhaps before many years, build up here mighty cities to rival Chicago, Cincinnati and St. Louis.

At Council Bluffs I met my Illinois friends with whom I expected to cross the plains; but here disappointment met me at the outset. Their companies were already full. I had been informed that as this was considered the "jumping off place," there was always someone to back out, but this time allurements were too great. All determined to go. On our trip up the Missouri I had formed the acquaintance of a bunch of Illinois teachers, men with whom I now entered into an agreement, but some rupture in their party changed the arrangements and I was doomed to a second disappointment. My next contract was with another Illinois man who was also a passenger with us up the Missouri. We soon purchased a team, but during our days of delay in getting outfit, provisions, etc., he was struck with a panic at seeing the immense tide of emigration flowing westward. His mind had never come to realize the vast extent of our western regions

and he felt assured that this multitude would crowd
that country to overflowing and to starvation; that there
would be such a famine as was never before known.
With these dark forebodings he declined the adventure;
wished he had not come and that he was at home again
with his mother. With this state of affairs there was
nothing left for me but to buy him out and send him
back to his home, where I trust he will ever remain. The
thirst for gold had lured him from home for this, the
first time, but hope and courage were not strong enough
to carry him thru. I was somewhat chagrined at this,
a third disappointment, yet I rejoiced that our rupture
occurred then and there rather than after a month's
travel on the plains, as has been the sad experience of
many, we are told. Partners have started good friends,
but when difficulties and dangers and hardships were
encountered they have disagreed and serious results
have followed. It was a trite saying, "If there is any hog
in a man's nature the bristles will show on this trip."

My next and fourth contract I never regretted. I had
the good fortune to fall in with David W. Culp and
James A. Hall. The former was a native of Pennsylvania
who had crossed the plains in '53 and spent eight years
in California mining regions and was therefore well
posted in western life. Being an active, energetic

character, of dauntless spirit, with a kind and generous heart, he was just the man for a companion in such an adventure. Our outfit consisted of two yoke of oxen costing $117.50, a wagon costing about $80.00, our bedding, consisting of buffalo robes and blankets, about six hundred pounds of provisions, consisting of sacks of flour, one barrel of hardtack, a few boxes of Boston biscuit, some bacon, coffee, sugar, dried apples, etc., cooking utensils, two revolvers and a rifle. On the 22nd of May, about five o'clock in the evening, Culp and I were prepared to "pull out," Hall to join us later by stage, and right joyful was I, after nine days of delay and disappointment, to find myself fully equipped and actually started on a journey which, though it appeared before me as mysterious and unknown as the journey to "the land of the hereafter," yet thrilled my soul with rapture. Never while my mind endures shall be taken from the art gallery of my soul the picture that met my gaze as we topped the first elevation and looked over that expanse of country—that boundless, undulating prairie—and never shall my soul forget that peculiar and indescribable rapture it experienced when I realized for the first time that I had passed beyond the bounds of civilization—beyond the permanent abodes of man— and was about to traverse a region where Nature alone has displayed her handiwork. My soul swelled as I gazed and my blood went thrilling through its channels. I was always an admirer of sunsets, but this to me was the sublimest I had ever witnessed as Sol slowly descended and at last sunk, as it were, into the bosom of the great prairie.

This first day we drove about six miles and camped about dark on a small stream. Our cattle were loosed from their yokes and left to roam and graze at liberty, while we partook of our repast of cold boiled ham, Boston biscuit and coffee, which to an Eastern epicure might be considered next to prison fare, but to us it was luxurious, though neither dainty nor diverse. Its novelty and our appetites gave it flavor. Our bed of blankets and buffaloes was arranged and we soon retired for a night's repose, which was calm, peaceful and refreshing—the first time in my recollection that I had slept out of doors.

May 23. Bright and beautiful. Started about seven, passed Elkhart near evening. Country rolling, hilly, picturesque. Numerous emigrants thronged the way with various styles of outfits, teams of horses, mules, oxen and cows. Many of the wagons had written upon their cover their place of destination in characters uncouth and spelled amiss. One among them, destined for the Golden State, had in legible though unsightly characters, "Kalaforny." Some of the wagons were attended by men alone, bound for some Eldorado where their dreaming fancies pictured their future fortunes, but most were attended with men and their families, women and children, starting out to seek new homes in the inviting states of the Pacific.

May 25. This was our first Sabbath on the plains, but its sanctity here, as on the river, was not much observed. One train alone we observed engaged in divine services.

We had a shower in the morning, accompanied by a perfect and beautiful rainbow. Our partner, James A. Hall, came up to us this morning by stage. Struck Platte River at North Bend soon after starting. This river, like the Missouri, is a turbid stream, but not so dark, more of a clay color. This condition is occasioned by the crumbling in of the banks, which seems to be a continual process; but unlike the Missouri, there is no "reconstruction," the soil being of a quicksandy nature; consequently the river is widening. What was its original width or what will be its ultimate dimensions—who can tell? At present it is from one to two miles wide and would not perhaps average over two feet deep. At first sight one would pronounce it a noble river capable of bearing upon its bosom the floating palaces that ornament and utilize our eastern rivers, but we find it scarcely navigable for more than an Indian canoe. Indeed, it seems peculiarly adapted to the necessities of the Indian and the wild beasts of the plains; while it waters a vast region of country, it offers but little obstruction to their journeying North and South. It is almost destitute of timber; few cottonwoods are found upon its shore and upon its numerous islands.

Passed the first Indian lodge this morning and camped in the evening near some others. Soon after camping five of the Pawnee tribe visited us on horse-back, begging for tobacco and whiskey, which, being peremptorily refused, they rode off to visit other camps. From various sources I had formed rather an exalted opinion of the wild Indian, of his physical development at least, "proud, noble, stately," which ideas, I must say, sadly and suddenly wilted down on my first sight of these red brethren. Of all the tribes we met on the route the Pawnees presented most signs of poverty and depravity, though they have been represented in the past as rather a superior race. If such was their primitive condition, the vices of civilization have sadly degenerated them.

The Pawnees are at continual warfare with the Sioux, and being an inferior race, unable to cope with them single-handed, they commit their thefts (which

is part of their mode of warfare), and retreat to the
settlements, where the whites defend them against the
Sioux. A short time before our visit the Pawnees had
gone up into the land of the Sioux and formed a treaty
with them, the first for thirty years; then, to complete
the contract, they stole fifty of the Sioux ponies and
returned to be protected by the whites. What wonder
the Sioux soon after broke their treaty of peace and
became hostile to the entire white race!

May 26. Left camp rather late; were passed by
Messrs. Houser and Carter, farmers from Illinois,
moving with their families to California. Reached
the crossing of Loup Fork, one mile from Columbus,
eighty-three miles from Omaha, about five P.M., but
were unable to get ferried till about dark. Camped
about one-half mile from crossing. A terrific thunderstorm with rain and hail raged throughout the night,
demolishing some of the tents of the emigrants, but,
in our closed wagon, covered with heavy duck cloth,
we felt as secure as in a house.

May 27. Started late and drove slowly to save the
cattle's feet, as slippery, muddy roads are very hard on
their unshod hoofs.

May 28. Started early—made twenty-three miles—
thunderstorm and heavy rain in night.

May 29. Next three days brought us to Platte Valley, opposite Fort Kearney—188 miles from Omaha.

June 1. Sabbath. Partner drove few miles in search of grass and water—rested cattle greater part of the day, which, as usual, was not much observed by emigrants. Sent to the fort for letters, but to my sad disappointment received none. The crossing of the Platte at this place is rather difficult. There is a large island in the river and the south channel is rather contracted and deep, yet fording is done with an ox team and large wagon, with waterproof sheet iron bed, the cattle swimming a short distance. Drove about eleven miles west of Fort Kearney. Passed one adobe hut, untenanted, the last vestige of white settlement on the plains.

June 2. Started early in search of game. After traveling about two miles over the bluffs returned without seeing antelope, deer or buffalo, though in many places buffalo bones in great numbers whitened the ground, showing that sad havoc had been made in their ranks by former emigrants.

June 3. Crossed Buffalo Creek, with steep banks but little water. Our afternoon road was over sandy bluffs. Saw numerous antelope gliding over the plains at such distance that their slender legs were almost invisible and their graceful bodies seemed to be sailing in the air.

16

June 4. Drove about twenty miles to one of the few places where, on the north side of the Platte, the bluffs approach the water's edge, leaving barely room for a wagon road between.

June 5. Drove a few miles and put up for the day to regale ourselves and cattle by the side of a small lake near the river. Spent the day comfortably and pleasantly and hoped to have spent the night the same; but as the sun went down and the wind fell a myriad of mosquitos came up from the lake and the marsh as if to repel our invasion of their domain and made such a furious assault upon us that we were forced to yoke our cattle and beat a hasty retreat back toward the bluffs. Finding no relief here, we again yoked our team and drove to Skunk Creek, about eight miles, by moonlight.

June 6. Passed Pawnee spring. Camped on the bank of the Platte. Mosquitos made another furious attack upon us, but we stood it out till morning.

June 7. Cattle driven off by mosquitoes; detained till about nine o'clock in consequence. Camped at nine P.M. on Buffalo fork, a fine stream, six rods wide, with sandy bottom.

June 8. Sabbath. Drove ten miles over a hilly, sandy road; put up for the day on Bluff Creek, upon which was a beaver dam recently constructed, in which was displayed much of the ingenuity and skill or that high order of instinct peculiar to these animals.

June 9. Traveled over about eleven miles of heavy road; thunderstorm in evening; rain and hail. Crossed several small but beautiful streams of water.

June 10. Nooned on Rattlesnake Creek, on the bank of which was a temporary trading post kept by a Canadian Frenchman, with whom I left a letter for home, to be mailed at the office on the opposite side of the Platte. Started about six P.M.—had a breakdown; detained a few hours. Camped about two next morning.

June 11. In consequence of late retiring the previous evening or, rather, morning, got out rather late this morning. Crossed Wolf Creek, a fine, clear stream; drove about twelve miles in evening; camped after night.

June 12. On turning out this morning found we had camped in the midst of a prairie dog town, which extended for acres around, with little hillocks denoting the entrance to their underground homes, and on which might be seen vigilant little sentinels yelping defiance or perhaps peremptorily ordering us to vacate the city. Travelers assure us that a species of owl and rattlesnake cohabit with these dogs, forming a peaceful family. I can vouch for the owl, which may be seen near the holes but the rattlesnakes I have never seen within or near the holes, though they are numerous on the plains.

A beautiful flower, somewhat resembling the morning glory, was in full bloom throughout the city. Drove about twelve miles to Platte river by noon; left about six P.M.; drove to one A.M. Crossed Shoal creek in the night.

June 13. A drove of antelope were seen across the river and two were seen upon our road. Drove till eleven P.M., when a heavy thunderstorm, accompanied with rain and hail, compelled us to camp.

June 14. Found ourselves this morning camped opposite Court House Rock, a peculiar formation of rock which in the distance so closely resembles the court house in St. Louis that emigrants from that place gave it the name it bears. Nooned opposite Chimney Rock, a noted landmark to ancient travelers on the plains, which so nearly resembles an immense chimney as to suggest the appropriate name it bears. This singular conformation consists of a conical elevation of about one hundred feet, its sides forming an angle of about forty-five degrees with the horizon; from the apex arises a nearly cylindrical and perpendicular shaft of about forty feet which has doubtless, from surrounding indications and from the testimony of travelers, been formerly much higher. Major Bridger is of the opinion that it was reduced to its present height by lightning or some other sudden catastrophe, as he found it had been reduced in height during his trip to St. Louis. Viewing it from the north side of the Platte it appears to be but a half mile from the river, but my partner, who had traveled the south road, assured me it was several miles distant, so deceiving is the eye in measuring distances in this level county and clear atmosphere. A violent gale came up in the evening; drove till half past twelve at night. Camped near Scott's Bluffs.

June 15. Sabbath. Drove a few miles in morning and laid up for the day. My partners had repaired to the river to attend to some laundry work, while I reposed upon a buffalo robe in the shade of the wagon. On this couch of comfort I soon fell asleep, from which condition I was suddenly aroused by a strange voice, but familiar salute of "How ! How !" I started up and before me was an Indian hunter, armed and mounted. His unanticipated appearance startled me for a moment, but a glance at his equipage and his mild and genial countenance, such as I never witnessed in another of his race, was sufficient to dispel any suspicion of hostility. He had packed upon his pony the venison of two deer which he had killed upon an island in the Platte where they frequently resort. We effected a "swap" with him. For venison we gave him an old white shirt, the long tail of which, flying in the wind, excited his mirth and tickled his fancy exceedingly. He was the first we had met, and a fair representative he was of the Sioux tribe; tall, straight and well proportioned; lighter in complexion than either the Pawnees or Snakes, with the most agreeable, mild and amiable countenance of any Indian I ever met.

June 16. Cattle missing; in our search met an Indian returning them. Whether he or the mosquitos drove them off we could not determine. Though strongly suspicious of the former, we recompensed him for his services with some sugar, of which Indians are exceedingly fond. Passed a French and Indian trading post; also an Indian village of seventeen wigwams. The squaws were busily engaged dressing hides; the papooses were wallowing in the mud by the river bank; while the men stood by the wayside gazing at us as we passed; from among them came the veritable Indian who returned our cattle in the morning with some half dollars to purchase sugar for his squaw. Camped after night near the river.

June 17. Nooned on the bank of the Platte. An Indian chief and his squaw came to us, begging provisions and presenting a certificate testifying that he was a "good Indian" and worthy of patronage in his profession of begging.

June 18. Found by the wayside a sign board upon which was written in characters uncouth, "Shmit Shop," and, our wagon being in need of repair, we drove down; found some Frenchmen occupying the shop and numerous squaws we supposed to be their wives engaged in making bead moccasins and other fancy articles. After making some purchases and procuring some milk, which cost us only the catching of a cow and helping ourselves, we drove opposite Fort Laramie.

June 19. Our partner, James A. Hall, had for some time been dissatisfied with our mode of travel, considering it dangerous, and had desired that we travel in a train, to which arrangement we, for various, and, we thought, good reasons, refused to agree. And as the majority rules, he had only to submit or separate from us. He preferred the latter; sold out to us his interest in the concern and joined a company for Carson City, California. In the afternoon I crossed the river in a skiff to Fort Laramie; was one day too late for an interesting scene—an Indian war dance. Returned in the evening; camped on Platte near Dry Creek.

June 20. Our friend, J. A. Hall, doubtless feels comfortably safe this morning under the protection of the train and we feel comfortably relieved by his withdrawal. A reluctant or timid companion on this trip is a great drawback, a great encumbrance, a heavy clog, a grand nuisance, beside adding much to our actual danger of attacks by Indians, as the best protection against them is a bold front. There were advantages, we thought, in traveling as we did—alone. We could make much better time, out-traveling many horse and mule teams; not being delayed camping and breaking camp, as large trains with women and children necessarily are. Again, we are able to keep our cattle in better condition. Large trains with families usually camp in regular camping places where wood and water can be obtained for cooking purposes; consequently grass becomes scarce and cattle must be stinted or be driven back sometimes a mile or more to the bluffs. This mile or two we preferred driving on the road, thus advancing us that much farther on our journey; and by carrying a supply of water and fuel we were prepared to camp any place where grass could be found. As regards danger, we felt we were as safe as in a train, for various reasons. We thought Indians would not steal oxen. Nine years before, when my partner crossed, they could be trusted to guard them for a slight remuneration. And we reposed in the belief that they would not consider our one little wagon worth robbing. Started about sunrise, buoyant, hopeful, resolute, for the journey; four miles

entered Black Hills; three miles farther brought us
to Cold Springs; seven miles more to Platte, making
fourteen miles of the roughest road we had traveled,
which made our cattle quite footsore for the first time
on the journey. Heavy gust around in afternoon; slight
shower; evening pleasant. This was a splendid camping
ground and numerous companies were here encamped,
resting their teams after the fatigue of the last fourteen
miles. In the quiet of the evening the sweet tones of a
violin brought to our desolate souls feelings of rapture,
combined with sadness. It carried us back to other
scenes; presented to our dreamy imaginations visions
of happy homes far away in the region of civilization.

June 21. Left camp early—road mountainous;
thirteen miles brought us to spring and ranch. Thunderstorm in evening; drove after storm about five miles and
camped after night in the mountains.

June 22. Sabbath. Drove about five miles to the river.
Mosquitos exceed anything we had yet encountered.
Violent hailstorm in evening; the largest hailstones I had
ever seen, many of them being nearly the size of guinea
eggs. Our cattle, when the storm commenced, were
grazing some distance from the wagon and, as is usual
with them, started and traveled with the storm, which
they will continue to do while it lasts. Fortunately their

direction was by our wagon, so we ran out and captured two and secured them to the wagon wheels; the others went on with the storm, but returned after it abated to their companions.

June 23. Roads muddy; did not break camp till about ten A.M. Took a stroll over the bluffs in search of game. Saw two antelope, but came onto them so unexpectedly to myself and them that they scampered away before I was able to arrest them. Saw, also, a jack rabbit or hare, which somewhat resembles a rabbit, but much larger; long, slender and light gray color. Very warm in afternoon; shower in evening; cool.

June 24. Roads mountainous, but not bad. Storm in evening.

June 25. Somewhat indisposed this morning for the first time on the trip. Prompted by the advice of an Illinois friend, I had brought with me a pint of brandy and some quinine for cases of sickness. Feeling that this was such a case, I prepared a dose according to directions, but found it so excessively-bitter I could not swallow it. Not being acquainted with either of the ingredients, I attributed the bitterness to the brandy. After adding quantities of sugar and coffee with the vain hope of making it palatable I threw the whole mess away in despair and disgust.

June 26. A cavalry company numbering about forty, with five wagons, passed down on the south side of the river this morning. Crossed Platte at old bridge; traveled five miles on south side to avoid sandhills on north; recrossed on new bridge; river being high, it was difficult gaining the shore from the bridge, the water coming into our wagon and wetting some of our goods. The mosquitoes for the last few days have been very troublesome, but at this crossing they made such an attack upon us as we had never before received. Drove several miles after night, hoping to get rid of them, but finding it hopeless and fearing our wagon would be broken by the frantic cattle, we camped and endeavored to relieve their suffering.

June 27. A few miles from camp, opposite Red Hills, our Mormon guide book informed us we would "Leave Platte River, to see it no more." Glad as we were to be advancing on our journey, yet those words brought to our hearts a feeling of sadness akin to that of parting with a near and dear human friend. For over one month it had been our friend and guide. Occasionally parted from it for a time, we the more appreciated its green banks and its cool, refreshing, though turbid waters. The stream at this place comes in from the southwest, while our course was directed northwest over a desolate

region of fifteen miles without grass or water, to
Willow Springs, with abundance of both, without our
accustomed pests—the mosquitoes. Three Indian
warriors of formidable and forbidding mien called upon
us in the evening, with whom we bartered some dry
goods for moccasins.

June 28. Four-mile drive brought us to a spring of
the best water we had met on the route—seven miles
more to Greese creek, where we nooned. Drove by
evening to Sweetwater; crossed on bridge opposite
Rock Independence. One of our oxen being lame, we
camped early. A company of soldiers were camped here
to guard the road from Platte bridge to Pacific Springs,
at South Pass. So much had our cattle improved on the
trip that the captain offered to trade us a sound ox that
had been sent them for beef for our lame one, which
was in better order, but our attachment to the animal
had become so strong that we declined the offer, hoping
for his future usefulness.

June 29. Sabbath. Showery—remained in camp.
Spent the day very pleasantly in reading and writing.

June 30. Went back about a mile to the military
camp with some letters. Found a man there in grief. He
had lost one hundred and thirty-five horses by Indians
the day before about fifty miles ahead. He had come

here for aid from the soldiers to regain his horses or to obtain redress. The soldiers stated that they could not move in the matter without orders from higher authority. As the telegraph between them and that authority was out of repair there was necessarily a delay sufficient to warrant safety to the Indians and to their pursuers. The unfortunate man also brought tidings of two men having been murdered by Indians on Sage Creek, some miles ahead.

Started early, but having a lame ox, drove but five miles and camped on Sweetwater, one mile past "Devil's Gate" one of the grand curiosities of the trip, a deep cleft in the Rattlesnake Mountain with perpendicular walls from three to four hundred feet high, through which the Sweetwater rushes. A remarkable peculiarity is that a few rods south of this cleft the mountain terminates abruptly. It is a problem for geologists how the river came to cut straight through the mountain instead of winding around its base at a slight grade, which was the course followed by our wagon road. A few miles south snow-capped peaks could be seen rearing their heads in noble grandeur and in bold defiance of the summer sun.

July 1. Drove eight miles and camped on the river.

July 2. About fifty soldiers passed by early this

morning. Came up with them in the evening and camped for the night.

July 3. Left camp early. The soldiers proceeded as an escort to the Governor of Utah, at his earnest request, to protect him from Indian hostilities. Drove about twenty miles and camped near a ranch that had been deserted the day previous on account of Indian depredations.

July 4. Started early—passed the graves of two men, James McGraw and brother-in-law, of Illinois, who had been murdered by Indians six days before, on June 28, 1862, as reported by the unfortunate horseman. Independence Day, like the Sabbath, was not much regarded as such, on the plains. In the afternoon a storm arose, with thunder and lightning, rain, hail and snow, clearing off in the evening cold as a November night, so that heavy blankets and a good fire were very agreeable companions.

July 5. White frost and ice about as thick as window glass. Started early and drove three or four miles before breakfast. During the day the sun shone quite warm, but the breeze from the snow-covered mountains was delightfully cool. In the afternoon I took a stroll up a mountain for a bucket of snow, which shone beautifully in a ravine near its summit—found there a huge snowbank gradually wasting away beneath the July sun, forming a delightful little stream of pure, cold water. Camped near the river on a small stream, near which stood a deserted stage coach and the wreck of a trader's wagon which had been plundered by the Indians a few days previous.

July 6. Sabbath. A passing stage this morning hitched onto the deserted coach and took it along. About six miles brought us to the junction of the old river road at the last crossing of Sweetwater, which old road we had left on the morning of the fourth because it was at this time impassable, as it followed the valley of the Sweetwater and crossed the stream at numerous points. which at the present high stage of water was unfordable. In the afternoon we crossed the dividing line between the waters of the Atlantic and the Pacific. I had received my idea of the "South Pass" in my youthful days from a picture in a school geography, where it was represented as a narrow chasm like the cleft in the Rattlesnake Mountain, through which rushes the Sweetwater, and I was somewhat disappointed in finding no such gateway. The summit is a smooth tract of country for some distance and so nearly level that the apex is indefinable by the eye alone. We were first conscious that we had passed it by finding the water flowing gently toward the setting sun. A peculiar sensation here stole over my feelings. Though beginning to realize with joy what for years I had had a longing desire for—to tread the Pacific slope— yet I could not step from the slope of my native Atlantic without casting one mental "longing, lingering look behind."

In this perilous region it is not safe that the heart dwell too much on home; it may soften by such reflections and become unfitted for what it may soon be doomed to encounter. We therefore smother in our breasts the impulse that would seek to rise and "drive back the tear to its fountain."

Camped in the evening near Pacific Springs, with excellent water and abundance of grass. From this place to Fort Hall is a new road—Lander's Cut-off—said to be shorter by eighty miles, with plenty of grass and water, in place of the desert traversed by the old road. The telegraph operator and keeper of the station informed us, however, that the road was perilous on account of hostile Indians and impassable from the unusually high water, without building boats and bridges. As we were not prepared for such business we felt doomed to the desert.

July 7. We were informed this morning that the Indians, during the night, had stolen some stock from the soldiers, quartered nearby for the protection of emigrants. What protectors!

which was done by erecting skids on a side hill, rolling the log upon them, one man standing on the log and the other in the pit beneath, and working the saw up and down, which was rather laborious exercise, particularly for long backs, but a determined purpose and vigorous health defied fatigue.

July 10. Day spent in cutting lumber, fishing, etc.; mountain trout are abundant in all the streams.

July 11. Having sufficient plank, we took our portion and started this morning for Green River. Soon after starting our eyes lit upon game—a large antelope quietly reposing near the roadside some distance ahead. I took my rifle and advancing cautiously upon "all fours" to avoid detection I hoped to get near enough for a sure shot, but the watchful creature was on the alert and either by sight or by smell detected my approach and sprang to its feet; but instead of scouring away over the plains as I expected, it started directly toward me, with an air of inquiry, but with cautious step. Fearing any moment it would turn and run and I should lose my prize, I took a rapid aim and fired, but must have been afflicted with what hunters call the "buck fever," for the creature, unscathed and unscared, still continued to advance. I hastily reloaded and with the "fever" at its highest pitch, feeling that it could not possibly stand over another second, I made another hasty shot and with like result. No one can know but from such experience my feelings of disappointment and chagrin as I watched its fleeting form scudding away to the mountains. By my target shooting I had acquired some reputation as a marksman, but now it was lost, and with it my much coveted game. One peculiarity of these animals is their curiosity. Hunters usually take advantage of this weakness by displaying a red handkerchief attached to the ramrod of their gun, while the animal, apparently curious to see what it is, advances till it becomes an easy prey.

About twenty-five miles of level, sandy road, for the most part, brought us to Green River at nine P.M.

July 12. Found grass abundant, but the mosquitoes so numerous and voracious that comfort for ourselves or cattle was impossible till the train arrived about two P.M. with their large herd of several hundred stock, which seemed to supply the demand for blood and we were, in a measure, relieved. This demonstrated why our sufferings with our four animals so far exceeded any-thing of the kind we ever heard of. Afternoon spent in building a flatboat. This was constructed of two sides—gunnels—about twenty feet long and two wide, rounded at each end and framed together; to the bottom of which was attached the plank, firmly pinned and calked with tow and pitch, which made it tolerably tight.

July 13. Finished and launched the boat by noon. Two boards were laid lengthwise of the boat, on the frame, upon which the wagons were run and one by one ferried over, which was rather a tedious process, as the force of the current and a strong wind down stream obliged us to drag the boat some distance up the shore before starting across in order to make the landing on the opposite shore. Crossed about a dozen wagons by night.

July 14. Crossed balance of wagons and swam the stock.

July 15. Loaded the boat entire upon two wagons and drove to west branch of Green River, about five miles distant.

July 16. Day spent in crossing. Partner sick; unable to be out of the wagon.

July 17. Having now passed the difficulties, as we thought, where we felt we needed the assistance of others, and realizing the others did not need us, we determined to pursue our journey alone. Although conscious that we were now approaching, if not already in the "enemy's country," that of the hostile Snakes, where from the start we had designed to connect

ourselves with a train for protection, yet our fear and
consciousness of danger had so worn away by familiar
contact with it that we felt no risk in venturing on alone;
in fact, we felt even safer alone than in connection with a
train. Our road took into the bluffs south of the ferry and
after a few miles was quite good. About a dozen wagons
"pulled out" with us. Nooned together on a small stream.
Towards evening encountered a large stream, deep and
difficult to cross; were obliged to wait for some horsemen
to explore it for the best crossing, then crossed over in
safety. The first wagon that followed while in midstream
broke an axle, but the energetic driver instantly grasped
and carried it in one hand, while with the other he drove
his team and brought the wagon with his family safely to
the shore amid shouts of applause. After crossing, train
camped for the night, but as our custom was to travel
later we secured water and fuel and drove till after dark,
making about four miles, and camped in the mountains
alone. This was a sad night for the friends we left at the
river in the evening. In the dead of night the Indians
came silently among them and ran off five of their horses.
Next morning they came in sight of the camp upon an
eminence a half mile distant, mounted on the stolen
horses. Five of the emigrants started toward them, two
mounted, three on foot, and as they advanced the Indians

fell back behind the hill, but when the imprudent men came to the top they beheld, as they represented, five hundred Indians, nearby and dashing upon them. The mounted men got safely to camp, but of the other three, one an Irishman named Moran, from Illinois, was shot through the heart; his son had an arrow passed through his forearm between the two bones, fell over some sagebrush, laid still and was left for dead; the third was surrounded and badly wounded with arrows. This threw the camp into such consternation that they neglected their stock and allowed them to wander away. A number of Indians rode around and drove off most of them. About two P.M. more horsemen came up from Green River and were about to make search for the thieves and stolen stock, but the women implored them to go first and see after the "Pennsylvania boys," as we were called, as they feared we had shared, perhaps, a worse fate. They followed to where we had camped and seeing we had left in the morning apparently undisturbed, they then set out for the Indians and found where they had killed and dressed an animal. Had they gone directly for them instead of for us they would probably have captured the party. This disaster very much crippled our friends for travel and obliged them to leave behind them many of their goods.

July 18. As we knew nothing of what had befallen our friends, we journeyed on, feeling confident that they were but a few miles back. Had we known our situation—our isolation—six days' travel behind one train and indefinite space before the other, we would, possibly, have shrunk from the danger that we knew surrounded us.

Crossed several deep and difficult streams during the day. In the afternoon the road entered the mountains and for a few miles was the most beautiful, romantic and picturesque we had met, as well as the roughest and most difficult to travel. Here we took a new road, cut through the woods on a hillside to avoid several crossings of the creek. On entering the timber the mosquitoes became intolerable which, together with an almost impassible road, made travel rather dangerous. Once our wagon was on the eve of oversetting as I threw my weight upon the wheel just in time to save it. Came to a bridge which was so narrow we deemed it unsafe to attempt to cross while the cattle were so frantic from the ravages of the mosquitoes; therefore camped for the night. During night a thunderstorm came up with a slight shower and a beautiful lunar rainbow appeared, the second we had seen on the route.

July l9. The road this morning was the roughest and

rockiest we had met; were obliged to stop frequently to rest our cattle. Passed a large snow bank with a peculiar red appearance which our limited scientific knowledge was unable to explain. A thunderstorm compelled us to camp early, though the place was almost destitute of grass; evidently the snow had but recently gone off and the grass was just starting.

July 20. Soon after leaving camp this morning we were somewhat startled on beholding by the wayside unmistakable evidence of Indian depredations. The first object was a trunk, open and empty. Nearby was the remains of a wagon and contents, the combustible portion of which had been burned. Amid the ruins were tools of various kinds, a whipsaw, gold pans, picks and shovels, etc., indicating a thorough outfit. Nearby were strewn books and letters bearing the name of John Campbell, Denver, Colorado Territory. Various other articles, as paper, candles, matches, etc., were lying around. A few rods farther, at the top of the hill, stood another wagon loaded with whiskey, and nearby was a newly made grave. All this we tried to construe into an accident—possibly death had occurred from disease or from accident—probably by the contents of the wagon, and that the stock had strayed away—anything to banish from our minds the idea of impending danger.

After gathering up such articles as we thought would be useful to us, we started on our way, but nearby found a large money belt clotted with blood. We then felt assured that foul play had been the cause of all and that we were really in a "scaly" situation. We had all along counted our chances of getting through as nine to one of being lost, but now we felt that the proportion was reversed. It was the first time in our journey that we had realized danger at hand, and knowing we were now in the heart of the Snake country, a tribe notorious for hostilities and a terror to everything west of the Rocky Mountains, it was not strange that a feeling like despair of ever again seeing our friends and home should, for a moment, steal over us. But though for a time we warily watched each tree and rock for a flying arrow, the annoyance of myriads of mosquitoes and the rough road we had to travel soon changed our feelings to indifference.

Passed over several large snowbanks that looked as if they might last till winter returned again. The scenery of today's travel was magnificent. Mountain peaks towering towards the skies, densely covered with evergreen trees, while by the wayside beautiful little flowers were springing into bloom, often within a few feet of huge snowbanks, but the continued assaults of mosquitoes, flies and gnats prevented us from viewing and appreciating Nature's grandeur as we wished. Wearied with the day's experience, we lay down to rest with as much indifference to danger as usual. Grass at this altitude was very scarce, but the water in these mountain streams, coming down from melting snow-banks, is delightfully cool and refreshing.

A few weeks later we learned the fate of Campbell whose grave we passed in the morning, from one who claimed to have been his companion. He was a trader from Denver, Colorado, with five others and two wagons so heavily loaded that on the hills they were obliged to double teams. They were bringing up the second wagon when sixteen Indians came out of the woods, greeting them in a friendly way and asked for "biscuit." Campbell, who was the only man armed, was in the act of reaching back in the wagon for something for them when they jerked his pistol from his belt and demanded the surrender of the party. Being helpless, they were obliged to give up. A peculiar fact with emigrants is, in the early part of the route, where there is no danger of attack, every man is "armed to the teeth," with revolver and knife hung to his belt, but when they get to the mountains, where there is actual danger, they have become tired of their weapons and

leave them in the wagons. After plundering the wagon
they ordered the men to strip off their clothing to their
drawers and then told them to run for their lives, which,
as soon as they did, the Indians commenced firing upon
them. Our informant on looking around saw the wool
fly from Campbell's cap and he walking quietly along.
He hallowed to him, "Campbell, why don't you run?"
then slipped into the woods and escaped with the rest of
the men to a train a few miles ahead. A number of them
returned and found Campbell dead. They buried him
by the wayside and left his wagons and contents for
the Indians or other emigrants. He informed us that
Campbell had with him $5,000 in gold. This, we feared,
might have been a temptation to his companions, and
as his tale was a little lame and he in bad company,
we strongly suspected him of being an accomplice in
the affair.

July 21. Drove till near noon—found grass in abundance, but the mosquitos in such superabundance that
our cattle were unable to eat, though they had been
fasting for several days. Partner being sick, we "turned
out" for the day. This afternoon was the saddest and
loneliest and dreariest of my experience on the plains
and put my courage and fortitude to a severe test.
I knew we were in the midst of hostile Indians.

My partner sick and almost helpless; I imagined my situation should he die, upon whose experience and wisdom and dauntless courage I relied in case of danger. The case of Campbell was fresh in my mind and gave rise to unpleasant visions and imaginations of the future; but knowing the effect of such upon my spirits would be unfavorable in case of actual danger, I summoned my combative spirit and determined to face, to the last, whatever might present, as the best means of safety.

Spent portion of time in vain endeavor to relieve our suffering cattle from the ravages of the myriads of bloodthirsty mosquitoes. No one can comprehend, from description, the amount of suffering those poor animals endured from mosquitos, flies and buffalo gnats. On parting the hair there was not a portion of their bodies that was not found covered with clotted blood, and after crossing deep streams the water running down from their bodies was deeply dyed with blood. Nor did we escape their violence. Blankets, without smothering, not even smoke, weren't any protection. The only time we could obtain relief or even opportunity to prepare and eat our meals with any comfort was during a strong breeze, sometimes toward the early morning.

July 22. Partner being better, we started early to avoid mosquitoes. Soon we descended the mountain into a beautiful valley, apparently about five miles wide and ten or twelve in length, with a strong but fordable stream flowing through it. Along its banks, at some distance, were two Indians, apparently hunting, and did not seem to observe us. Soon after we met four more mounted on ponies. As they advanced they did not hail us with the pleasant greeting—the kindly salute of "How! How!" as was the custom with all others we had met, but rode by silent and sullen, with an expression of countenance that told plainly they were not our friends. After going a few rods they halted, held a short council, then turned and followed us. The oldest of the four, we presumed about thirty-five, was decidedly the most hideous specimen of humanity I had ever seen. His countenance alone would have convicted him of any atrocity before any intelligent jury. A short upper lip, exposing his teeth and gums, gave him more the expression of a snarling bulldog than of a human being. All were armed with bows and arrows and some had small game they had captured. They rode up beside our wagon, as is their custom, and examined its contents. The oldest fancied our buffalo and insisted upon having it, but we were obliged to refuse. In the meantime two of the others had taken two ox bows from the wagon and hung them upon their ponies' necks, which delighted them exceedingly. As we did not wish

to spare them, partner went immediately to one and
demanded it, grasping the pony in one hand and the
bow in the other. The Indian held to it tenaciously till it
was wrenched from him; the other, seeing we "meant
business," threw his back into the wagon. The old Indian
then rode up beside me as I was seated in the wagon,
shook his head with a threatening air and a countenance
far from amiable, saying, "Indian mire! Indian mire!"
I "returned the chief his haughty stare," looking him fair
in the eye and giving a significant shake of the head,
which significance a loaded revolver in hand aided him
in comprehending. It had the effect of changing the
expression of his countenance from a bold, haughty
threat to that of a collapse. They then renewed their
demands of the buffalo, pointing up the valley and saying,
"Heep Indian, heep Indian," as if to intimidate us. This
was answered by pointing back and saying, "Heep
wagons." Becoming satisfied they could not prevail
upon us to give up the buffalo, they withdrew a short
distance and held another council, after which the oldest
started away across the prairie at full speed and soon
disappeared, while the others followed quietly after us.

This maneuver produced with us some misgivings—
some dark forebodings of what might follow. Thus far
we had maintained our courage and kept a bold front,

but at this moment, I admit, our hope almost gave way, though our determined spirits remained unshaken. While we did not, in the least, fear these four, we did not know but four hundred might be close by, whose hands were yet stained with the blood of the unfortunate Campbell, whose grave we passed only two days before. Though we were, in principle, peace men—non-combatants, under certain circumstances— yet under the present we felt we could not afford to be non-resistants. Though our motto was "Peace on earth and good will to all men," our watchword was "Go through or die." When the warrior on the battlefield faces danger and death he knows that if he falls his body will receive an honored burial and his name and his fame be rendered immortal. Under such circumstances men have deemed it a glorious thing to die. But when in an obscure recess of the Rocky Mountains an ignominious death confronts him—death at the hands of rude savages, where his body, perhaps, may remain as food for the prairie wolf and his bones be bleached by the elements, the event is not so glorious.

About a mile from where our savage friend left us we saw him again, by the roadside, some distance ahead, awaiting our approach. We found him in a more amiable mood, having a number of half dollars and desiring to purchase our buffalo. Not knowing what kind of climate we might yet encounter, but judging from the snow-covered mountains around us that we would need the buffalo, we were obliged to positively refuse disposing of it upon any consideration. They finally ceased their entreaties, though evidently dissatisfied, and next asked for matches, which we freely gave them, and they rode off apparently as well pleased with what they had obtained as we were to get rid of them. They were by far the most unruly wretches we had yet encountered and fully sustained the reputation of the Snake Tribe. We had some suspicions that they might come upon us in numbers that night and obtain by force what they could not by moral suasion, and therefore kept somewhat on the alert—"slept on our arms"—but passed the night unmolested.

July 23. Started early—roads tolerable, but mosquitoes, flies and buffalo gnats almost intolerable. Found a tree blown across the road which we were obliged to cut away. Soon after we found the fresh tracks of a large bear which had been coming towards us, but had here left the road and taken to the brush, evidently alarmed at the sound of our ax. I had a curiosity to see the animal and was anxious to look him up, but my partner did not favor the enterprise, but advised me to leave him alone if he was willing to leave us alone, and assured me we would find in him a more formidable foe to encounter than the Indians. He was evidently of enormous size and weight, as his broad feet made more impression in the road than did the sharp hoofs of our oxen. He appeared to be on a pedestrian tour to distant parts, as the tracks continued in the road during a half day's travel. What would have been the result had we met face to face is a problem we are satisfied remains undemonstrated.

Camped at the head of a large valley opening on a lake. Mosquitoes exceed in number and size anything we have heretofore met. This we christened "Camp Misery."

July 24. Left soon after daylight to avoid mosquitoes, which we found very bad till afternoon, when a breeze arose, which relieved us. Crossed a large stream in the evening and camped upon its banks—the first peaceful camp we have had upon the cut-off and which we named "Camp Comfort." An old Indian hunter passed us today.

July 25. Started rather late—crossed several deep streams; road good, but dusty. A young Indian hunter passed us today. Could speak some English and was very polite and sociable. His intelligence and civility contrasted widely and favorably with his brethren we had passed a few days since. Came onto the old emigrant road in the evening, to our infinite satisfaction, making nineteen days on the long-to-be-remembered Lander's Cut-off, upon which I experienced more hardships, more exposure, more danger and more misery than ever in my life before; but now that it was passed we rather looked back upon it with satisfaction and pride, as well as with gratitude, for our safe deliverance.

July 26. Roads very dusty; passed several Indians with berries for sale, who were very kind and friendly.

July 27. Sabbath. Drove about two miles, when to our great joy we beheld a camp of twelve wagons. They were fragments of other trains that had crossed Snake river; some with a view of crossing the mountains to Salmon River gold mines; others designing a shorter route to Oregon via Fort Boise. They had been lying there for near a week in a state of indecision. They declined taking the northern route on account of its expanse and uncertainty and were afraid to proceed on the lower from fear of danger, having heard that the Indians were in force about fifty miles ahead and were murdering and plundering trains. In this dilemma they were awaiting other trains to strengthen their force. When we came up to them with our "little ox train" of one wagon and informed them that we had traveled thus from the Missouri river and purposed thus to proceed next morning, some counted us rash, reckless and foolhardy, while others seemed to feel ashamed of their timidity. We laid up for the day to rest ourselves and cattle and to enjoy the pleasure of looking again at white faces—Caucasian at least—they being the first we had seen for ten days.

July 28. Took in with us two Englishmen, William Uren and son, of Mineral Point, Wisconsin, who had lost their horses by Indians two weeks previous and had given their wagon to one of the train to take them and their goods through, but being tired of delay and anxious to travel, were willing to leave their wagon and go with us; and we being tired of loneliness, of seeing no white faces but each others, were glad of their company. As we drove off, leaving our timid friends, they bade us goodby with the cheering remark, "When you get cleaned out we want that wagon." Soon after we left them, however, they concluded they would be about as safe traveling as lying there and so "pulled out" and came up with us that night. Road today dry and dusty and country very barren. Two horsemen overtook us on their way from the ferry of Snake River to that of Portsmouth, a few miles ahead, on our route.

They pretended much friendship—pulled out a bottle and desired us to drink, which we respectfully but positively declined, my principle and practice being "total abstinence," and they, my partners, being suspicious that all was not right with it. They seemed somewhat astonished, if not offended, at our want of civility in refusing their hospitality and so left us. Arriving at the ferry in the evening, we found the same two men who had passed us during the day. They seemed to be partial proprietors of both ferries, here and on Snake River. Here, too, we found the gentleman who claimed to have been the companion of Campbell, and gave us the account of his murder. The only other white man about the concern was an old Mormon. He cautioned us against traveling alone, saying the Indians were very bad on the road and that we were in danger of losing our cattle and our lives. My partner in his rash, imprudent way replied, "If the white men will only leave us alone, we are not afraid of the Indians." This was too much for the old man, too strong an insinuation, and either from a guilty conscience or an extremely sensitive nature he took it as a gross insult, which he resented, and an altercation ensued which the bystanders feared would become serious; so he refused to give any further information respecting the road.

My partner was unquestionably right in his belief that were it not for the white traders and outlaws who were among the Indians, leading them on to depredations, emigration could pass through unmolested, but it was certainly unwise and imprudent thus to make the bold assertion and "beard the lion in his den." Nine years before when he passed through to California the Indians could be trusted to guard the cattle for a slight remuneration. They would always steal horses, but horned cattle they had no use for.

July 29. Met a man today, Mr. Young, with pack mule, who was fifteen days from Salmon River; was on his way to meet some friends. He and his partner had been attacked by Indians about one hundred and fifty miles ahead and robbed of their horses. In the conflict he received eight arrows in his body, one barbed arrowhead still remaining in the clavicle. Had it struck a half inch higher or lower it might have entered a vital part and proven fatal. He exhibited his wounds and related his adventure with as much coolness, and, indeed, apparent enjoyment, as if the whole affair had been a pleasure game. And as we examined the arrowhead carefully, for fear of inflicting pain, he said, "Take hold of it; don't be afraid; you can't hurt me; I'm an old Californian!"

July 30. Cold and windy. Passed the falls of Snake River this morning, about thirty feet high, rough and rocky. In the spray that rose from the surging foam was a beautifully tinted rainbow, and upon an isolated rock in mid-stream a wary eagle had made her aerie.

July 31. Roads heavy—country dry and barren. Nooned on a large stream, near the banks of which was the grave of G. W. Sanders, who died four days before. Finding no water in the afternoon, drove till about midnight to a spring near an extensive marsh.

August l. Found fresh Indian tracks nearby, where he had evidently been prowling around our camp. Left in the afternoon, drove about eight miles and camped on a pleasant stream. Twelve packers from the gold mines bound for the States, camped near us. Their approach caused some alarm to the train which, at the time, happened to be a little in advance of us. When they saw them advancing and discovered they were horsemen they concluded they must be Indians and that they meant hostility. Their captain ordered a halt and preparation for defense, which is made by forming the wagons into a corral, as a kind of fortification to protect themselves and cattle, but when they approached they discovered to their infinite satisfaction, that they were friends. From their diary we obtained much useful information respecting the route, its camps, etc.

August 2. Left early—drove twelve miles to creek by noon—twelve miles in afternoon. Camped near the river. A mustang pony that had been left at this camp by the packers on account of disability was then taken possession of by the captain of the train and afterwards sold to one of the company for five dollars. She was supposed to have been bitten on the leg by a poisonous snake, which disqualified her for service. After a few weeks, however, she recovered and became a very serviceable animal—tough, hardy and sure-footed.

August 3. Windy, dusty. Drove twelve miles to stream by noon; eleven miles in the afternoon to Antelope Creek. This is a winding stream of moderate size, shut in by a beautiful hedge of green willows, with plats of excellent grass in places along its course, which contrasted favorably with the dry, dusty, barren region we had been traveling over. We turned our cattle out to luxuriate in a fine grass plat, triangular in shape, shut in on two sides by the stream and on the third by the road. Our custom had been, after the cattle had fed, to bring them up near the wagon to lie down, and, when in dangerous or suspicious places, to tie two of them to the wagon wheels, but this evening, before we were ready, they had lain down and were reposing so comfortably in the tall grass that we disliked to disturb them, which proved to be an unfortunate mistake, as was revealed by daylight next morning.

August 4. On looking for the cattle, which was my morning duty, I found they were gone, strayed or stolen. As there was a train camped about half a mile back, we had some hope they had gone to them, but on inquiry this hope was blighted. I then returned to seek their trail, which I found crossing the road with the tracks of four Indians, all leading northeast in the direction of Snake River. We had heard that two tribes were united north of Snake River and were plundering trains on the emigrant route. Thinking that was their destination and that our only hope of recovering the stock was to capture them before they crossed the river and joined their band, I rushed to the wagon, got my revolver, requested partners to procure horses, if possible, from the train, while I started immediately in pursuit. After going a short distance in the direction of Snake River the trail turned southward, crossing our road of yesterday and proceeded straight for the mountains. Before reaching them I was joined by one of our new comrades, the son, and soon we came onto a pair of cattle belonging to the neighboring train. Being old, they were usually left out of the corral. They had both been shot with numerous arrows in a vain effort, we presumed, to make them travel up with ours, which were young and active, but finding them too slow they abandoned them. An arrow was still lodged in the side of one of them. On extracting it we found the barb had been broken off.

On entering the bluffs or mountains the trail followed up a deep, dark cañon for some distance, then took to the highlands. Here we found some spots where fire had consumed the grass, apparently the night before. We presumed it had been lit to direct the steps of the flying thieves. Thus we pursued the trail as best we could over rugged mountains till noon, making, as we thought, about twelve miles from camp; as far as we would be able to return by night; and as the Indians had a decided advantage of us, in the way of a start, and we being sometimes delayed by losing the trail, we reluctantly and with sad and heavy hearts gave up the pursuit as hopeless. It was indeed a painful moment when the last faint hope expired of ever recovering our team, which by long association and faithful service through hardships and sufferings indescribable had endeared themselves to us as much as is possible for dumb brutes to be endeared to human hearts. Not only so, but to the traveler on this route, at this distance from the settlement, his team is his life, as it were, or as essential to it as is the ship to the mariner in mid-ocean; therefore it is that danger of losing it makes him desperate.

Having had neither food nor drink all day and feeling keenly their need, we directed our course westward, which we knew would strike the creek upon which we were camped, somewhere in its course. On arriving at it, however, we found ourselves apparently several hundred feet above it, with an almost perpendicular descent to the valley below, through which meandered the beautiful belt of green willows, with here and there the silvery stream appearing to tempt and aggravate our thirst. We followed down the bank for some distance and found a gulch which wound its way down to the valley and through which we made our way with some difficulty, at times jumping down a perpendicular jog of several feet, not contemplating what would be our fate should we encounter fifty feet or more and be unable to return. We soon slaked our thirst with pure, fresh, sparkling water as it issued forth from the rocky chasm. Here also we found some wild currants, which were very acceptable after our long fasting. We journeyed on down the valley and towards evening came out into the open plain about a mile from camp. Wearied and footsore we rejoiced that our

journey was so near an end and felt that another mile
would be more than we could endure; but on rounding a
point in view of the camp ground what was our
astonishment, dismay and chagrin on beholding the
whole place deserted, not a wagon or human being
remaining. A few crows and prairie wolves, the gleaners
of deserted camps, were the only occupants of the
place. Feeling confident that our companions would not
thus leave us voluntarily, we were at a loss to account for
their disappearance, when we discovered a card upon
which was written, "Boys, you will find us at the next
station." This rendered the problem even more inex-
plicable, as the next station, we knew, was ten miles
distant. Why did not the same card inform us of
some provisions suspended in a certain tree, for our
sustenance, knowing that we left without breakfast or
provision? My query was, "What had become of Dave,
my partner, whose warm heart was always more mindful
of others' necessities and comforts than of his own?"
Slightly incensed at this heartless outrage, as it now
appeared to us, we laid down upon the bank of the
stream to rest our wearied limbs and to muse over the
past and uncertain future, and feeling unable for ten
miles more, we decided to remain there till morning.
But as we mused our displeasure grew to violent

exasperation, the stimulating effects of which seemed to give us strength for the emergency; so, after eating some berries which we had brought for our friends, but found we had no friends for the berries we renewed the weary tramp. About ten P.M. we came up with the train, encamped on the bank of a large stream. Our feelings of indignation toward them were somewhat changed when they came crowding around us with hands of welcome extended and with showers of comments and congratulations. They offered many earnest apologies for leaving us, saying they had no idea we would ever return or that they would ever see us again in this world. They did not suppose we were fifteen minutes in that dark cañon before we were killed—they felt that no efforts of theirs could save us, and that the best thing for their safety was to leave. To console my partner, however, they agreed to remain at this camp till noon next day; if we did not then appear they would go on and leave us.

The history of their day's experience is this: Soon after we left, my partner, another man of the train about eighty years of age, and two young men, one on foot and the other on horseback, followed after us to the foot of the mountain, when a smoke arose which set the whole party in consternation, it being the Indians' signal to call their warriors together, as they explained. The two young men rushed back to camp, leaving my partner and the old gray-headed man to take care of themselves. The teams were harnessed and the train started, thinking the Indians would be immediately upon them. As they passed our wagon my partner remonstrated with them for thus leaving us helpless and alone to the mercy of the Indians, and in his irrepressible vindictiveness upbraided them for their cowardice. Unable to resist such suasion, they halted till near noon, their teams remaining in the yokes, when another smoke arose which sent an electric thrill of terror through the train. They immediately manned their teams and started, regardless of my partner's appeals. They would not stay, but offered to take our wagon with them to the next station, which favor, after much hesitation, he accepted, old man Uren going with it, but my partner remained, looking for us until toward evening.

This day's travel was the heaviest tax on my physical strength I had experienced on the plains—such a tax as I could not have endured but for my greatly improved health and strength. After partaking of a wholesome supper we reposed our wearied limbs upon our buffalo, spread upon the ground in front of the

corral, and soon the day's experience was in oblivion
and we in the arms of Morpheus. About twelve o'clock
we were aroused by the cattle rushing out of the corral
in rather close proximity to our quarters, and men
rushing to and fro in wild confusion. Heard someone
inquire, where is the guard, and the reply, he's been
shot. They seemed confident that the Indians were upon
us—had shot the guard, stampeded the cattle and
would soon slay us all. Their excessive cowardice
made them apprehensive of every imaginable danger
and disaster. On springing to my feet I saw the horses
standing quietly at their pickets, which was conclusive
evidence that Indians were not about, so I returned
to my lowly couch and was soon wrapped again in
peaceful slumbers. The whole disturbance was soon
assigned to a trivial cause—a man stepping out of his
wagon in deshabille.

Some weeks later we learned how much danger
we narrowly escaped in our rash endeavor to recover
our cattle. A large train camped at the same place was
attacked at night, the guard shot and cattle stampeded.
The next day a party of twenty-two men went in pursuit
and after following about twenty miles, as they judged,
eight more than we, they came upon a large camp of
Indians with great herds of horses and cattle—doubtless

the stolen property of many unfortunate emigrants. The Indians came forward and defiantly told them to come and get their stock in plainer English than Indians are accustomed to speak. After a few shots between them the whites ceased firing and while holding a consultation whether to make a desperate charge the Indians charged upon them and all but five fled. These stood their ground and deliberately fired upon the advancing foe till one of their chiefs fell and was carried off by his companions. As the owners of the stock were the ones that ran away, the braver five concluded not to further peril their lives and so quit the field, leaving the property in the hands of the Indians.

August 5. We were now left helpless and dependent, though not despondent, as we felt that we had many warm friends in the train left on Lander's Cut-off July 17, which we supposed was close behind, not knowing at that time that they had met with a worse disaster and were unable to help themselves. As our company, or rather our assistance, was desirable to the train we were with, they arranged to take us with them. One emigrant from Nebraska, Perry Watkins, whom we shall ever hold in grateful remembrance, very kindly furnished us two yoke of his best cattle from his own team, yoking some cows to make up his team, while others of the train relieved him of a portion of his load. Thus ended our comfort and pleasure of this trip. From this on we were obliged to endure the dust and discomfort, the delay and inconvenience of traveling in a train. The dust in this country was very dry and light and deep and the prevailing northwest wind brought it back, a perfect cloud, in the faces of those in the rear, till their happy countenances were scarcely recognizable. That justice may be done to all it is the custom for the rear wagon one day to go in front the next, so we were allowed one day's comfort in thirteen. I found the train had brought along the old ox from whose side we had taken the arrow, but on learning his condition they shot him. Started in the afternoon, drove about five miles and camped on same stream.

August 6. Drove about ten miles over a dreary, desolate region, where the only signs of vegetation was the inevitable sagebrush, and nooned upon Snake River, where the banks were very steep and high, down which the cattle were obliged to wind their way to the water. Grass was very scarce, even in the river bottom. The whole country presented an air of desolation and the sullen river, shut in by massive, rocky walls, with no sign of living beast or bird, reminds you of "that lake whose gloomy shore Skylark never warbled o'er."

On the opposite shore, near the river's edge, was a pool of water, blue as indigo, in whose rocky bed was, no doubt, deposited some mineral which may some day be developed for the benefit of mankind. Camped at night near the river—grass very scarce.

August 7. Passed several Indians with fish which they wished to "swap" for fishhooks. They inquired anxiously if there were "heap wagons" on the way, seeming desirous of a market for their fish.

Crossed Salmon Falls River in the afternoon and camped near its mouth. A number of Indians spent the evening about our camp. They were the smallest of stature and the most destitute class we had met. One old chief presented several fearful scars on his breast which he said he received in his youth in battle with the Snakes.

August 8. Left camp about sunrise—passed Grand Rapids, on the Snake—roads hilly, sandy and dusty. Camped after night near the river.

August 9. Drove eighteen miles over heavy, dusty roads and camped on the river. A number of deserted wagons were on the grounds—doubtless some unfortunate emigrants had lost their teams and were obliged to abandon them. Portions of them had been taken away by other emigrants, as is the custom of the plains, a deserted wagon being counted public property, and anyone being privileged to appropriate a wheel, a tongue, a bolt, or whatever will serve his purpose better than his own.

August 10. Drove seven miles in the afternoon.

August 11. Drove fourteen miles on the river.

August 12. Mr. Watkins lost one of his finest oxen this morning by snake bite or from alkali.

August 13. Road principally on river bottom and tolerably good. Two men with wagon and three packers camped with us. One of them had crossed the plains to California some years before and gave us some interesting incidents, among which was the capture of a white man in Indian paint and costume. One morning their camp was alarmed by a band of Indians charging upon them. In the contest that ensued one of their chiefs was wounded in the thigh; fell from his horse and was captured. His captors proceeded to wash his face and found a white skin disguised beneath the paint. He claimed to be a Mormon, but could not be made to say that Brigham had any knowledge of or had anything to do with his present business. They were at a loss to know how to dispose of him and were about to leave him in his helpless condition to the mercy of the next train, but one of their party, "Old Man Gilmore," whose family had been murdered about this same place one year before, could not consent to pardon one who might have been the perpetrator of the bloody deed—he placed a revolver at his head, turned his face away and fired—killing the unfortunate desperado on the spot. This may seem like unwarranted severity, as there was no proof that he was guilty of the crime for which Gilmore took his life. Be he guilty or innocent of that particular act, he was guilty of that which is doing much today to keep up hostilities between the red and the white races—was in league with hostile Indians, leading them on to depredations for which the Indians receive entire blame and perhaps chastisement. There is little hope for the Indians until these outlaws are removed from among them, and the first step for government in its attempt to civilize them is to arrest and bring to grief every white man cohabiting with them and not engaged in some legal, "visible means of support." The Indian is perhaps by nature somewhat prone to evil, but by education far more, and that education from the race whose influence should be to elevate and purify rather than to drag down and corrupt.

August 14. As we nooned today by the side of the river an Indian sat upon a rock on the opposite shore, viewing us in silence. One of our men remarked what a

pleasure it would be to take his rifle and put a ball
through him and see him drop over. Inhuman wretch!
Though a fair representative of the class of whites in
immediate contact with the Indians, who regard them
as no more than the wild beasts of the mountains, and
do not hesitate on slight provocation or for mere amuse-
ment to shoot them down, which outrage is avenged,
not always upon the perpetrator, but upon the first
white man who unfortunately falls in the way of the
exasperated friends of the murdered Indian; this again
is returned by an attempted annihilation of the whole
tribe or race. Thus it goes on, crime following crime and
blood paying the price of blood, and thus it will until
the golden rule can be instilled into the hearts of the
savage red man and the worse than savage white.

August 15. Started about daylight and drove ten
miles to Current Creek soon after noon—grass good.
Some horsemen—mountaineer bandits, we strongly
suspected—camped near us.

August 16. Road today over mountainous country;
drove till late at night, hoping to find grass and water,
but were obliged to camp without either.

August 17. Sabbath. Drove three miles to river by
daylight—grass good—camped for the day.

August 18. Started at two A.M.—reached small

stream soon after sunrise, where we halted for breakfast.

Drove to the river by ten A.M. and camped for the day that our cattle might recruit, as the frequent fasting, the dust and fatigue of heavy roads was fast exhausting them.

August 19. Started at three A.M.—drove ten miles on river—crossed two streams flowing from hot springs near the road. Had twelve miles in afternoon of heavy, sandy road—camped on river.

August 20. Left about three A.M. Met three hundred soldiers on the road eastward to meet and assist emigrants. Camped on the river.

August 21. Left at three A.M.—drove till near noon without stopping, when we crossed the Owyhee River and camped upon its bank. A spring of excellent water issued from its bank, which was very refreshing and highly appreciated in this parched region. A Mr. Clark, an old Oregonian, of Umpqua valley, nooned with us. He was on his way eastward to meet some relatives who were emigrating to Oregon. From him we obtained much information and advice concerning the country and our journey. He advised us to cross the Cascade Mountains by the wagon road south of Mount Hood, to save the expense of going down the Columbia River by boat or trail, which advice, however, proved unfortunate to us, as the loss of stock from exposure and hardship was greater than the expense by the other route. He told us much of the customs and habits of the people of Oregon—that girls married usually at fourteen, frequently at twelve, and in one instance at ten—that eighteen is the dividing line between a young and an old maid—that there was but one unmarried girl in the state past twenty-one years of age, and that was his own daughter. By what means she escaped the inevitable fetters so long he did not inform us.

August 22. Left camp at one A.M.—drove twenty miles to Malheur River and camped on a small stream near by. Several packers with a number of ponies, bound for Salt Lake, camped near.

August 23. Started late—drove six miles to Sage Creek by noon—six more in afternoon—camped near, by Sulphur springs.

August 24. Sabbath. Left camp at daylight— drove ten miles to Snake River by noon, four miles in afternoon brought us to Burnt River, to which we had been anxiously looking forward, as we were promised good camping and abundance of grass.

August 25. Road runs up the river—very rough and mountainous. Camped in valley—grass good.

August 26. Road continues up the river—mountainous, but good. Ascended one branch of Burnt River and crossed over the mountains to another, upon which we camped.

August 27. Crossed numerous streams, tributaries of the Burnt—roads tolerably good for the mountains.

August 28. Our road today was up a long and steep ascent crossing the water shed of Burnt and Powder rivers, from which elevation the scene around was most magnificent; mountain peaks towering up in all directions, with valleys and gorges between, while Powder River Mountains, with snow-covered peaks, adorned the Western view.

August 29. Started about daylight. The scenery today was grand, as we descended the mountain into Powder River valley, a beautiful, level and fertile tract, about six miles on each side of the river. Crossed the stream, its turbid waters giving evidence that miners were at work upon its mountain tributaries, and camped upon the west side of the valley.

August 30. Partner started early for the gold mines. Drove about two miles and camped upon a small stream, Pine Creek. Found these small streams, rushing down the mountainside to the river, abounding with salmon, working their way up stream, and which we found were very easily captured. Shot three in the evening, one of which weighed eighteen pounds.

August 31. Sabbath. Very warm—remained in camp.

September 1. Light shower—heavy wind in the evening. Emigration is pouring into the valley, some locating and claiming tracts for farming, others prospecting through the mountains for gold deposits, while others, not pleased with prospects here, are going farther. We had learned before reaching here that Salmon River mining was a failure and that miners were coming from there to this place; that, though reports were true in regard to its richness, that one man had taken out $3,000 in one day, Yet the extent was limited to about three miles, and the rush of adventurers so great that five thousand men were in the place without employment. This excitement, though it brought sore disappointment to many, was a favorable thing for the country. It brought in thousands of enterprising miners who, though disappointed, were not discouraged, but proceeded to prospect and develop new territory.

September 2. Went this morning to Auburn, the mining town of Powder River, distant about ten miles from the valley. It was my first visit to a mining town; and, as it was dignified with the term city I was somewhat disappointed in its extent and appearance. The houses were chiefly of log, some of canvas, and extended for a few hundred yards along a muddy stream upon which was the principal mining. Saloons and gambling dens were well patronized, but a lack of water for mining purposes caused a general stagnation of other business. The mines were thought to be rich, but without water they could not be worked. A ditch was being dug, but the prospects for water this fall were not very promising. Hundreds of idle hands were depending solely on the drift of fortune for their winter's subsistence. The price of provisions was: Flour, twenty cents per pound; bacon, thirty-five cents; sugar, three pounds for a dollar; coffee, fifty cents; beans, forty cents, etc. After viewing the city to my satisfaction and thinking of it as Cowper of the *Peasant's Nest*, "Let it be my visit, but never mine abode," I returned to the valley, repeating to myself Goldsmith's poem of Auburn—the "Deserted Village"—suggested to my mind by my idea of the prospective future of this village of the mountain.

September 3, 4, 5, 6 and 7. Spent in the valley recruiting our stock upon the luxurious grass that abounded there and ourselves upon the luxurious salmon we caught in abundance in the streams.

September 8. Mr. Watkins and family leave this day for the Willamette Valley and I, being tired of gypsy life

and desirous to get once more into the region of
civilization, engaged to go with them, but my partner,
feeling that the mountain region was the only place for
him, determined to stay and take the hazardous chances
of the mines. We therefore dissolved partnership, shook
hands and parted. Four months of association, through
pleasure and suffering, through perils and hardships,
had bound us together as brothers. I realized from the
first how greatly I was dependent upon him for the
wisdom he had acquired by experience, but not until by
my own experience did I fully realize what his had been
worth to me. While everyone seemed to think us insane
or natural idiots to travel alone, yet had it not been for
his determination to do so the trip no doubt would have
been to me, in point of health, more damaging than
beneficial. While alone we had every day the pure,
invigorating air of the plains and the mountains, on the
other hand, with a train, we would have been breathing
dust every day except the few on which it would be our
turn to lead. We separated with deep regrets and with
many kind and earnest wishes for each other's future
welfare. Drove a few miles and camped for a small
stream—grass abundant. This valley gives, evidence of
great fertility and would doubtless yield a rich reward to
careful culture.

September 9. Started early—roads rough and dusty. A young man traveling on horseback, alone, to Walla Walla camped with us.

September 10. A large elk, the first we had seen, came near our camp. Met a number of Indians moving with their families and stock. They present rather an amusing, if not ludicrous appearance. Upon a small pony will be mounted an enormous squaw, with a papoose before and one behind. To another will be attached, on either side, a number of lodge poles, the hinder end dragging upon the ground and between them is suspended a kind of hammock, containing one or more papooses. The road soon left the valley, taking a westward course across the mountains. About noon we descended a long, steep and rugged hill into Grand Ronde valley. This is apparently a fine, level and fertile valley extending about five miles in either direction. Camped on western side.

September 11. Road leaves valley up a steep and rocky hill—the first ascent of the Blue Mountains, over which we have forty miles of the best mountain road we have met. Met a number of Indians with their families. They are civil, well appearing and apparently well off in ponies, dogs and papooses.

September 12. Passed a small spring in a dry creek

bed which our cattle soon exhausted. An old Indian meeting us here, just too late for the benefit of the spring, turned away with an indignant air, muttering, we presumed, vengeance upon our cattle. Nooned on side of the hill; found water half a mile down a deep ravine. Camped in open space on the top of the mountain.

September 13. Cloudy, rain at noon, the first we had had for a month and a half.

September 14. Sabbath. Cloudy in morning— clear at noon, when we descended a long but easy slope to the valley of the Umatilla. The view of this valley from the mountain as we descend is one of the most beautiful we have witnessed, as we look down upon its broad expanse, with a streak of beautiful green willows meandering through it where flows the Umatilla. Called in the evening at the Indian agency, over which floated the stars and stripes, the first we had seen for three months. There was something unusually inspiring to us in those colors at this time and in this place. In the vicinity the Indians are engaged in farming, are well clothed and appear well off. At this time they were about gathering their corn. Camped about two miles down the river. Cool and fall-like.

September 15. Heavy frost in the valley. In a few miles crossed Umatilla River, a clear, wide, but shallow stream. Met here a trader with apples, the first we had seen, for which he was asking twenty-five cents apiece. Three miles farther we came to a small settlement. Crops look well; land appears very productive. From here the road takes to the highland and for twenty miles is destitute of water.

September 16. Passed another small settlement today; crossed large stream and after thirteen miles of sandy road camped on small stream.

September 17. Seventeen miles of dusty road brought us, after dark, to a spring of filthy water. No grass.

September 18. Drove few miles before breakfast to grass. Crossed Willow Creek in the evening. Camped in highlands.

September 19. Eighteen miles of good road brought us to a spring of fine water; two miles more to Rock Creek, where we camped for the night.

September 20. Cattle having strayed away, did not get started till near noon. Drove six miles to John Day's River, a broad, clear stream about two and one-half feet deep, with stony bottom. Finding no grass, drove to the highlands up a very steep and difficult hill. High wind all night. Air cool and fall-like. These highlands abound in a peculiar growth of grass called "bunch grass," growing in scattered tufts or bunches, very thick and fine, which at this time of the year, though perfectly dry and dead appearing, is very much relished by cattle and is said to be very nutritious, fattening stock in a short time.

September 21. Left the Walla Walla and Dallas road and took the one for the mountains. Drove fourteen miles to a ravine, camped one mile up. Grass good.

September 22. Drove all day in ravine, road good, grass abundant.

September 23. On leaving the ravine this morning we came in full view of the Cascade Mountains, numerous peaks of which were beautifully white with snow. Mount Hood, towering above all others, is an ornament to this entire region and a landmark to travelers. Camped on a hill near DeSchutes River.

September 24. Descended a long, steep and rocky hill to the river, where a bridge had been constructed across the chasm, through which rushes and dashes the foaming stream. A number of Indians were camped on its rocky shore, engaged in catching and curing salmon. This is done by spearing them as they ascend the falls and drying them upon the rocks. Ascended a rocky ravine and camped near its head.

September 25. Horses being lost, were detained till noon. A friendly Indian went in search of and found them for us. On inquiring his charge for the service he replied, holding up six fingers, "Six pony, six dollar." After some dickering he abated somewhat from this demand. Drove six miles in the afternoon to Tygh Valley, a fine, fertile tract of a few miles extent, with one village of six or eight families, having two stores and two smith shops.

Ascended a long and steep hill from the valley; drove nine miles; camped on a small stream; windy, cold.

September 26. Being stormy on the mountains, we remained in camp, as it is not considered prudent for travelers to attempt to cross while Hood hides his countenance, as he did this day, behind dark clouds, which occasionally lowered toward the valley. Wind high and cold all day.

September 27. At three miles passed Barlow's Gate at the foot of the mountains. This is the commencement of a journey of eighty miles over the Cascade Mountains, a road almost entirely destitute of grass, cattle being forced to subsist upon bushes, and in many parts laurel is so abundant and so fatal to stock that they are rushed through all day, fastened up in a corral at night without feed and again rushed through next day till danger is passed.

September 28. Sabbath. On descending Laurel Hill, one of the steepest and most difficult descents of the

Cascades, an accident occurred to one of our wagons which detained us several hours. So steep was the descent that the wagon bed, not being sufficiently secured to the axles, slid forward over the oxens' backs, injuring one somewhat. Persons unacquainted with mountain roads could scarcely credit their description; or seeing them would not believe it possible for wagon and team to go down without all being demolished together; and their passage can only be effected by removing all but one yoke of cattle, and rough-locking all four of the wheels, or as is frequently done, by attaching a tree top behind the wagon to drag after and hold it back. One peculiarity of these mountains is that the eastern slope is gradual; you ascend a cañon or ravine to the summit with but little difficulty, but the western side is abrupt and rocky. This same feature is a peculiarity of the entire American continent; the Atlantic shore is low and sandy, sloping gradually to the Alleghanies, while the Pacific shore is precipitous.

Drove a few miles up Sandy Schouts River and camped with but a slim supply of grass or bushes for our stock.

September 29. Rain in afternoon. Camped at *Summit prairie;* grass abundant, but ground very miry. Two men camped with us, one of whom lost two horses at this place a few days before in a snowstorm.

September 30. Rain and snow. Started this morning,
hoping to reach a ranch, twelve miles distant, but
various disasters so detained us that we were obliged
to camp in the mountains without grass or water, save
what was furnished in puddles by the rain and melting
snow. This was the gloomiest night I had seen on the
mountains or on the plains. Rain and snow had been
falling all day and we were wet throughout, and hope of
reaching the ranch was gone. Night was upon us, dark,
dismal and cold. We built a log fire, which I kept up all
night and stayed by, preferring such quarters to a bed in
the wagon with wet clothing. This day and night's
exposure brought on again my throat trouble, the first
I had felt on the trip, which, except for this too great
exposure, I might never have felt again.

October 1. Morning revealed the fact that a number
of our horses were missing, which we had supposed
were with another wagon at the summit of the hill. We
found their tracks going back and presuming they were
bound for summit prairie, our previous camp, where
there was good grass, I mounted a pony, Cayuse Indian,
and started in pursuit. The snow was falling thick and
falling fast, but melting partially as it fell, making it wet
and disagreeable. I found it deeper as I ascended the

mountain, till at our nooning camp on the previous day it was about four inches. I was pressing on with all speed for summit prairie when suddenly my pony threw up her head, brightened her countenance, quickened her step and endeavored to quit the road and take off through the woods, which at first I forbade, but finding she so earnestly persisted in her way, I gave her the rein and soon, at a few hundred yards, we came upon the group of horses, huddled together, where they had apparently been standing most of the night. From this incident I learned to trust the intelligence or "high order of instinct" of dumb animals, for the sagacity of this faithful Indian pony saved its horse companions from perishing and saved us hours of toilsome and perplexing search and exposure. One fine American mare we never found, but presume she perished.

Started from camp near noon for the ranch, yet seven miles distant; one horse and three cattle gave out on the way from exposure, fatigue and starvation. Were obliged to leave two wagons and proceed with the stock to the ranch, which we reached after dark. As we descended the western slope of the mountains magnificent scenery presented itself. The mountaintops were covered perfectly white with snow, while their base was richly decked with deep dark green of pine and fir, the

line of demarcation between the pure white snow
and the evergreen trees, those "emblems of purity
and immortality," being very definite and keeping its
level from peak to peak. This night, October 1, was the
first we had slept under roof since leaving Omaha, May
22. Our domicile was an open shed with a blazing log
fire just outside. Thus housed, with our buffaloes, and
blankets spread upon the ground, our sleep was sound,
peaceful and refreshing.

October 2. On waking this morning, to my great
astonishment, I found a woman asleep by my side and
her husband next beyond. They were hardy mountaineers who came into camp and "turned in" after my
companions and I were asleep. Rain. Two men went
back for the wagons that were left behind. In the afternoon a young calf, which had probably been lost from
some train and allured by our cattle, came near our
camp. As such stock is counted game here, I took my
rifle and deliberately and unscrupulously put a ball
in its brain.

October 3. Still rainy. Drove a few miles—roads
very muddy—camped on the bank of a large stream;
grass very scarce.

October 4. Rain, as usual—roads slippery. About
noon the sun came out and promised fine weather; but

soon the clouds gathered and the rain poured down again for a few hours. I very much regretted the cloudy weather, as the scenery over these mountains, in fair weather, is said to be sublime, Mount Hood's snow-covered peak adding grandeur to the scene, but which, owing to the mist and fog, we saw but once, looming up before us like a giant snow bank, and appearing but a quarter mile off, though the nearest point, we afterward learned, was four miles distant.

Reached the Mountain House early in the evening, where we were kindly treated by the proprietor, who generously requested us to go into the garden and help ourselves to fresh vegetables without money and without price, a privilege and a luxury we highly appreciated, being the first we had seen for months. This is rather a favored spot—a clear, fertile spot of land on an elevated ridge of the mountain, with grand scenery around and, but for the solitude of the place, would be pleasant for a long sojourn.

October 5. Sabbath. Spent this as a day of rest, but not of fasting. Fresh beef, new potatoes and green peas were largely indulged in, while our wearied cattle enjoyed the luxurious grass and the day's repose.

October 7. Drove five miles to next ranch, kept by an old Frenchman, who had here made for himself a comfortable home in the midst of the mountains, planted fruit trees and was now reaping the reward of his labor in an abundant crop.

October 8. Rain in the morning. Mr. Brown and family, who had been our traveling companions for weeks past, left us today, taking the road for Oregon City. Drove six miles and camped in a prairie of fern of prodigious growth. A soil that can produce such growth of vegetation will doubtless some day astonish the world with its mammoth fruits and vegetables.

October 9. Two miles brought us to Foster's, at foot of mountains, making twelve days in crossing the Cascade Mountains, a distance of eighty miles. Here we found a finely improved farm and buildings that much resembled those of a Pennsylvania farmer. Camped one mile beyond on Eagle Creek.

October 10. Frost in the morning—clear and pleasant during day. Horses having strayed, drove but one mile and spent the day in fruitless search.

October 11. Frost, clear, pleasant. Found our horses, but too late to move camp.

October 12. Sabbath. Crossed the Clackamas River in the morning. Country a mixture of timber, brush and prairie. Vacant houses and abandoned farms were numerous by the way, giving evidence of defeated enterprises, as on the banks of the Missouri River. Drove about twelve miles and camped on highland, with deep ravine on either side.

October 13. Three miles brought us to Cutting's Mills. On inquiring here "what is the latest from the seat of war," we were informed, rather sarcastically, that "in recent battles the Union troops were defeated, losing sometimes one, sometimes one and a half, sometimes two, but always retreating in good order"; from which we inferred that our informant was a "reb" at heart. Crossed Molalta Creek and prairie and passed the first school house we had seen in the state. Camped on the property of Mr. Van, about twelve miles from Silverton.

The next few days, to October 18, were spent in locating the Watkins family on a farm he had secured. And thus ended, this day, a chapter in my life's history which I shall never regret having passed through nor ever desire to repeat.